PERSONAL PRAYERS

FOR MOTHERS

A PERSONAL PRAYER BOOK

PERSONAL PRAYERS
FOR MOTHERS

Brief meditations and prayers
dealing with experiences and feelings
common among mothers

Nancy J. Nikolai

DIMENSIONS
FOR LIVING

PERSONAL PRAYERS FOR MOTHERS

Copyright © 2004 by Dimensions for Living

This book is printed on acid-free paper.

ISBN 0-687-35104-9

04 05 06 07 08 09 10 11 12 13 — 10 9 8 7 6 5 4 3 2 1

MANUFACTURED IN THE UNITED STATES OF AMERICA

To my dearest and most precious blessings:
Ross, Sarah, John, and Abby

BEING A GODLY EXAMPLE

Teach [these words of mine] to your children, talking about them when you sit at home and when you walk along the road, when you lie down and when you get up. —Deuteronomy 11:19

Dear Lord,

Sometimes I focus so much on *caring* for my children, I forget to be proactive in my other roles as a mother. Help me remember that you have placed me in my children's lives as an example, a t*eacher* and *mentor,* as well as a caregiver.

Please give me discernment to recognize opportunities for "teachable moments," whether it's as we are driving in the car or as we are waiting in line at the grocery store. Give me the wisdom to know what to say at such moments. Keep me close to you through prayer and reading your Word, so that when opportunities for learning and sharing come, your precious words will flow through me to my children. In Jesus' name. Amen.

FOR MY CHILD'S SALVATION

That if you confess with your mouth, "Jesus is Lord,"
and believe in your heart that God raised him from the
dead, you will be saved.   —Romans 10:9

Dearest Lord Jesus,

I thank you that you are my Savior and that you
have drawn me to you. I am a new creation because
of your transforming power and love.

I ask that you would begin to stir within my child
the desire to know you and to be known by you.
Help her not only believe in you, but trust and
obey you as well. May she desire to stay in the cen-
ter of your perfect will every day of her life.

As she comes to understand the importance of
seeking your forgiveness for sins, may she also realize that your Son, Jesus Christ, has paid the penalty
for each and every one. Amen.

We Are Never Alone

For I am convinced that neither death nor life, neither angels nor demons, neither the present nor the future, nor any powers, neither height nor depth, nor anything else in all creation, will be able to separate us from the love of God that is in Christ Jesus our Lord.
—Romans 8:38-39

Dear God,

Thank you for being our shepherd, friend, and companion on this journey called life. We never have to face trials, temptations, or stressful times alone. Give my children courage in knowing this. Impart to them the security of knowing that you will never leave them or forsake them, nor can anything separate them from your incredible undying love.

Teach my children how to draw from your limitless strength during difficult and lonely times. May they turn to you first, instead of to people or things.

Help me remember to relate examples of your faithfulness to my children so that they will be able to draw encouragement from these examples when they need them. Thank you for being *Jehovah-Raah,* "The Lord Our Shepherd." Amen.

Not Ashamed

I am not ashamed of the gospel, because it is the power of God for the salvation of everyone who believes.
—*Romans 1:16*

Dear Lord,

You are so precious to me, and I never want to hurt you or bring dishonor to your glorious name. I pray that my children would have this same heart toward you and desire to please you in all they say and do.

When they are faced with a situation in which they are tempted to deny knowing you, give them the courage, wisdom, and faith to stand strong and to identify themselves as yours, unashamed. I pray that, in a gentle and loving way, they would be a witness to those who are lost and hurting. Give them the right words to say in particular situations, and show them when it is best just to turn and walk away.

If they do deny you in some way, may they always ask your forgiveness and know that just as you forgave Peter, you will forgive them. Make their faith strong so that they can stand in times of testing. Amen.

FOUND OUT
WHEN GUILTY

"You may be sure that your sin will find you out."
—Numbers 32:23

Dear Father,
I recognize that you are omniscient, knowing all things, and I praise you for this attribute that belongs to you alone. As the Bible says, "You understand our thoughts from afar." (See Psalm 139:2.) Oh, how this holds me accountable!

I pray that when my child is doing something wrong, you will let him be found out and will help him realize that there are consequences to sin. Stop him while it is still a thought. Help him think it through and know that you love him too much to let him get by with it. May he accept your discipline, whatever form it may take. Protect him from habits that can become detrimental to him.

May he also remember that he has a mom praying for him to get caught in wrongdoing! Let him be thankful for that some day. Amen.

STRONG PRAYER LIFE

Do not be anxious about anything, but in everything, by prayer and petition, with thanksgiving, present your requests to God. —Philippians 4:6

Dear Lord,

The old hymn says, "What a privilege to carry everything to God in prayer." It is indeed a privilege to know that the Lord of everything, the King of the universe, cares about my every need, no matter how big or small it may seem. Thank you, Jesus.

Let my child understand the importance of prayer. Help me model this by coming to you when my child has a problem and praying with her over that situation. Let her see me studying your Word and "catch" me having a private prayer time. Help her understand the importance of developing her own personal prayer time, but also to realize that she can turn to you at any time and all times with her worries and concerns, her joys and triumphs. May she have peace in her life as she communes with you every day.

Keep her focused, guard her heart and mind, and help her prayer life to grow as she draws closer to you. Amen.

BUILDING FAITH

And we know that in all things God works for the good of those who love him. —Romans 8:28

Dear Lord,

Sometimes things don't happen the way I had hoped, prayed, or planned. I wonder, *Why me?* as I see things unravel before my eyes. But no matter how bad things may seem, you have always been faithful.

Help me demonstrate my faith to my children during these trying times and remember that they are watching. In times of doubt, may I be filled with your grace and wisdom; in times of testing, may I be filled with your perseverance and strength; and in pain, grant me your peace and comfort. Build their faith through the transparency of my life. Amen.

Learning Disabilities

"For I know the plans I have for you," declares the
LORD, "plans to prosper you and not harm you, plans to
give you hope and a future."   *—Jeremiah 29:11*

Dear Lord,

I bring my concerns for my child's learning disability before you, knowing that you understand what she is going through so much better than I do.

Sometimes it is hard to know how to help her. Please give me wisdom to know the things I should do, such as providing helpful suggestions for the teacher, exhibiting understanding and patience when working with her, and knowing when to recruit help from other qualified professionals.

Bless my child's relationships with her teachers, and grant them the attentiveness, care, and encouraging words they will need as they work with her.

Let us all work together as a team to propel my child toward a bright and hopeful future. Strengthen her through these trials, and increase our faith in you.

Thank you, Father, for your goodness and your incredible plans for her. In Jesus' name. Amen.

INDEPENDENCE

You hem me in—behind and before; / you have laid your hand upon me.   *—Psalm 139:5*

Dear Lord,

As my children face each new era in their lives, I face new eras in my parenthood. I think back to when they were toddlers just learning to walk, and how I would try to protect them from those inevitable falls, holding my hands in front of and behind their little wobbling bodies.

Now, as I see them skipping into new territories, wide eyed and naive, I pray that you would place your mighty hand in front of and behind them. Keep them on your path, protecting them from as many "bumps and bruises" as possible. Amen.

GIVING WITH JOY

They urgently pleaded with us for the privilege of sharing in this service to the saints.

—2 Corinthians 8:4

My children watched as the little girl opened their gift to her. They were visiting an orphanage for the first time. As the little girl saw the doll and stroller, she showed no reaction, but her beautiful brown eyes twinkled. My children asked, "Mom, why isn't she smiling?" I told them, privately, "That may not be how she shows joy."

It made me ponder the reason I give gifts. Do I give for selfish motives, expecting something in return, or at least the payment of a smile for my efforts?

I later explained to the children that we give out of the outpouring of love that you have given us through your Son, Jesus Christ. Thank you, Lord, for your precious gifts, which you unselfishly lavish upon us. Amen.

Idols of Today

"Therefore since we are God's offspring, we should not think that the divine being is like gold or silver or stone." —Acts 17:29

That's an idol!" my perceptive nine-year-old announced. He was in the midst of watching a show with his little sister and noticed the way the character was talking about an object. Thank you, Lord, that he understands what an idol is.

It seems that my teenager is the one having a hard time with this concept right now. As he strives to model his life after someone, let him be drawn to your example. Protect my children from bad influences, and bring other strong Christian mentors into their path along the way, whether it's a teacher, an older teen from church, or a relative. May they always worship you, the Divine One, instead of the "divine" things you have made. Amen.

FEELING TREASURED

*But we have this treasure in jars of clay to show that
this all-surpassing power is from God and not from us.*
—2 Corinthians 4:7

Dear Lord,
I thank you that you are our counselor. When my
child told me that she was not invited to be in a
classmate's "club," you know how my heart went
out to her. How can I help her understand what a
precious treasure she is to *you*?

I know she will go through significantly more
painful times than these. Impress on her heart the
promise that, as long as she clings to you, she will
never be crushed, forsaken, or destroyed. Walk with
her through lonely times; let her feel your presence
and know that it is your power that will guide her
through. Amen.

COMMUNICATION

What you heard from me, keep as the pattern of sound teaching, with faith and love in Christ Jesus.
—2 Timothy 1:13

It is so hard to turn off the radio when I'm driving the kids somewhere. Although my preference is to listen to my favorite station and just "veg," there are so many opportunities I miss with my children when I don't take that time to touch base, to connect, or just to laugh with them.

Lord, I don't want to relate to my children in a hit-or-miss fashion. Remind me to be proactive in expressing my interest in their lives. Amen.

First Date

You have sincere love for your brothers, love one another deeply, from the heart.

—1 Peter 1:22

Here we go!" I said, with a grin, to my husband after our beautiful oldest daughter informed us she had been "asked out." Before giving our consent, we called a family friend who knew the young man. Our friend reassured us that this boy was a good kid.

O Lord, please give us wisdom about what rules and boundaries to set up to protect our child without suffocating her. Help her make wise choices and set her own boundaries for dating. I pray that she will base her decisions on the faith and values and self-respect that we have tried to instill in her. Oh, and I pray my husband will not intimidate the poor boy too much when he shows up at the door! Amen.

Miscarriage

Be with Christ, which is better by far.
—Philippians 1:23

It was the second time we had gotten our hopes up. (And that is an understatement.) We were ecstatic about having another child! As my belly began to grow, I became excited and thought, *This pregnancy will be different. I've made it longer than I did before the miscarriage last year.* So my husband and I decided to tell our children, family, and friends. Then the spotting began, and once again the ultrasound revealed that the baby's tiny heart was silent—not beating. As my husband and I held each other and cried, we silently tried to prepare what to say to others when we were desperately searching for answers of our own.

Thank you, Lord, for the prayers on our behalf prayed by your people, some of whom we didn't even know. Our faith remained strong, even though we went through all kinds of feelings, including anger. Help us continue to trust you as so many of our questions go unanswered. Amen.

Bad Behavior

Let us examine our ways and test them, / and let us return to the Lord.   —*Lamentations 3:40*

Dear Lord,

When my teenager threw a fit today, it reminded me of when he was two years old and would test me to see if I would give in after that type of behavior. It didn't work then, and I need to get across to him that it will not work now either. Help me keep my composure when he acts out of control. I sent him to his room so both of us could calm down, and then I discussed with him later why his behavior was wrong. Privileges were taken away, but he accepted his punishment with an apology, which I quickly accepted.

Please help me be firm and yet fair with all my children. May my children truly be repentant when they do something wrong. I also need to be consistent in my discipline and follow through when I say I will do something. Please let me decide on the consequences for bad behavior with love, not anger. Amen.

SELF-DISCIPLINE

He who works his land will have abundant food, / but he who chases fantasies lacks judgment.

—*Proverbs 12:11*

Dear Lord,

I know that self-discipline is a trait that is so important for my children to have. But it is not something that is inborn or easy. It is learned through training and example.

I still struggle with this in some areas of my life. Please show me which habits hinder me from modeling this quality to my children. Let me continue to make improvements according to your Word, not the world's advice. Let me remember, though, that I am constantly in the process of becoming more like Jesus, and I need to be patient with myself as well as with those around me—especially my children. Amen.

SICKNESS

Each of you should look not only to your own interests, but also to the interests of others.
—Philippians 2:4

The flu season is upon us, and it seems that everyone around us is getting the bug. Dear Lord, please protect us from getting sick. I thank you for our health and give you the glory for it.

When I do become ill, it's so hard. It seems that everyone else can take a sick day to recuperate, but not *Mom*. Help my family be more attentive when I'm sick. Help them understand that I need a break from work in order to recover. May they do their part to keep the house in good shape, keep the laundry up, and, at least temporarily, take care of themselves. May we all learn what it is to be a servant when someone is sick, even if that someone should happen to be *Mom*! Amen.

RESPECTING OLDER ADULTS

In the same way, you who are younger must accept the authority of the elders.   *—1 Peter 5:5 NRSV*

Dear Lord,

I know sometimes it is hard for children to be patient with older adults. They sometimes are slower physically and can be hard to communicate with.

The generation gap can also cause young people to choose entertainment, perhaps, over sitting and listening to a senior citizen.

Help me model patience with older adults wherever I am—visiting an elderly family member, in the grocery store aisle, on the highway as I wait to pass. When it comes to older adults, help my children become excited about hearing the stories that they have to tell, the experiences they've had, and the way things were when they were younger. Let my children value those who are elderly as treasures, wise people from whom we can learn so much. Place special older people in their lives for them to get to know. Amen.

MATURITY

And Jesus increased in wisdom and in years, and in divine and human favor.   *—Luke 2:52 NRSV*

I've heard that if you don't teach your children responsibility when they are young, they have to learn it the hard way, through experience. Maturity grows from the lessons children learn through having responsibilities, and sometimes that includes allowing my children to face the consequences of their choices, right or wrong.

Lord, please grant my children wisdom, maturity, and the desire to please and love you more and more. Let them read your Word and be grounded in it. Let me pass wisdom on to them in the everyday situations of family life. May my children always feel comfortable coming to us and to you with their problems and questions. We know your Word says that you gladly give wisdom to those who ask. Thank you for wanting to share your great wisdom with us. Amen.

A LARGE FAMILY

Then little children were brought to Jesus for him to place his hands on them and pray for them.
—*Matthew 19:13*

Lord,

You know how deeply I love each of my children. The first reaction some people have when finding out I have four is, "Wow! *Four* kids?" My husband and I have always wanted a large family, but the reactions of others can sometimes be negative. It can even cause me to feel anger when people express these negative opinions in front of my children.

Help me be patient with those who do not understand and to forgive them. Never let my children think they are just one in the crowd or that they are a bother to us. To me, they are not "those four kids"; each is a precious individual with his or her own gifts, talents, and perspectives. Our life is so rich because of them, and my husband and I are so blessed. Thank you, Lord, for the privilege of being their parent. Amen.

My Husband's Needs

However, each one of you also must love his wife as he loves himself, and the wife must respect her husband.
—Ephesians 5:33

Dear Lord,

Thank you so much for my husband. He loves me and our children so much. But he also needs our love and support in return. There are so many times I get so busy with the house, with work, and with taking care of the children's needs that I fall asleep as soon as my head hits the pillow.

My husband sometimes needs focused communication and intimacy. May I be careful not to show a nonchalant attitude toward him in either area.

Help me build him up by complimenting him, listening to him attentively, and showing him that he is the most important person, besides you, in my life. Give me the time to take a short nap during the day if I think he will need to spend more time with me that evening. Please continue to bless our marriage and protect it. Amen.

FUTURE SPOUSE

Therefore what God has joined together, let no one separate. —*Matthew 19:6 NRSV*

When I first found out I was pregnant with our first child, I began to pray for his future spouse. I did this with all of my children, and I continue to do so to this day. It is one of the most important prayers to pray for my child. The person each one marries—if that is God's will—will profoundly affect who he or she will become in the journey through adulthood. Their spouses will also affect what kind of people my grandchildren become.

Lord, may you have your mighty hand on my children as you guide whom they date in preparation for selecting the person they marry. Keep them and their future mates pure in their bodies, minds, and hearts. May they be raised by loving parents who love you and who encourage them in their relationship with you. Give my children wonderful love stories. Amen.

SAFETY AT SCHOOL

Therefore be as shrewd as snakes and as innocent as doves. —Matthew 10:16

Dear Lord,

In recent years there have been so many instances of schoolchildren coming into harm's way. Having children in both elementary school and middle school, I pray you would keep them all safe.

Bless them with authorities in their lives who will make wise choices in decisions that will affect my children and the other children for whom they are responsible. Heighten their awareness so that they may recognize potential dangers and be able to prevent them.

May your loving, yet powerful, protection surround the schools my children attend, and bless everyone in their perimeters with peace, acceptance, and the joy of learning. Amen.

SUMMER ACTIVITIES

The LORD will watch over your coming and going / both now and forevermore. —*Psalm 121:8*

Dear Lord,

School has just let out, and the children and I are so excited about all the plans our family has made for summer vacation. Bless this time that we have together. Don't let us become so busy that we forget to have "lazy days" when we just hang out and do nothing!

Keep us safe as we go on our family vacation. Be with the children as they go to church camp and sports camp. Protect them from injury and harm at all times. Thank you for this wonderful time of year. Amen.

TRANSPORTATION SAFETY

He gathers the lambs in his arms / and carries them close to his heart; / he gently leads those that have young. —*Isaiah 40:11*

I received the phone call on my cell phone. The school secretary hesitantly said: "Uh, Mrs. Nikolai, there has been an accident. One of our buses was involved in a crash this morning. There were only minor injuries, and your two children seem to be all right, but we want you to come by and make sure." My heart went to my feet. Never did I expect to get a phone call like this. I took it for granted that my children would safely arrive at and return from school.

Lord, please protect my children every day whether they are on the bus, in the carpool, in our own vehicle, or even just waiting for me to pick them up. Keep us safe at all times as we travel to and from our destinations. Thank you for protecting my children, each and every day. Amen.

Puberty

"... so that you may be able to discern what is best and may be pure and blameless until the day of Christ ..."
—*Philippians 1:10*

My two oldest children are only a year apart, and both are in the beginning stages of puberty. My son, the oldest, is growing very quickly, beginning to speak deeper with an occasional crack in his voice, and is growing a small mustache, which he is very proud of.

My daughter is also growing by leaps and bounds and is maturing more every day. She and I have had "the talk" about the changes her body will be going through in the next few years.

I can't believe these years are already here! They grow up so fast. Please, Lord, give my husband and me the wisdom and courage to talk to our children in a discreet, matter-of-fact, and nonembarrassing way about the changes they are experiencing. Give them discernment in knowing truth from falsehoods, and may they always be comfortable coming to us with any questions or concerns they may have. Amen.

Overcoming Temptation

Those who belong to Christ Jesus have crucified the sinful nature with its passions and desires.

—Galatians 5:24

I remember being taught that we strengthen either the Spirit of God within us or the fleshly nature within us. For example, when I read God's Word and pray, I am building up the spiritual nature and becoming more like Christ.

I pray, O God, that my children would be strong in their convictions and their faith in you. Don't let them be influenced by ungodly activities around them. When they are confronted and sometimes bombarded with temptations, give them the words to say, if they need to say anything, and help them get out of that situation as quickly as possible. Help them always feel that they can talk to us about any issues they may face. Amen.

Being Their Advocate

. . . keeping a clear conscience, so that those who speak maliciously against your good behavior in Christ may be ashamed of their slander.   *—1 Peter 3:16*

My child came home one day and told me his teacher had done something that was unfair and embarrassing to him. The "mother bear" in me came out with claws bared, ready to go to my child's defense.

Lord, at times like this, help me cool down and come to you. May I not show disrespect to my child's teacher, but show him it is okay sometimes for people to disagree. Help me show self-control and not react out of anger. Help me work with the teacher to solve the problem without putting the teacher on the defensive. Give me wisdom and the right words to say. Make the teacher's heart soft and ready to listen to my concerns. May my child know that I'm on his side and he can come to me when he feels something is wrong. Amen.

ACTIVITIES

Remember your Creator in the days of your youth.
                                        —Ecclesiastes 12:1

When all four children were involved in two or more after-school activities each, my husband and I quickly became overwhelmed. We knew some of the activities had to go, but they all were such great opportunities for our children, it was hard to decide which to give up. Even though we felt strongly that our children should see their commitments through, we needed to have more time for our family.

Lord, please continue to give us wisdom about what to do about activities for the children. We want their lives to be enriched, and we don't want their talents to go to waste. However, we also don't want our family time to be sacrificed. Thank you, Lord, for the good gifts you give us. Amen.

FINANCES

Dishonest money dwindles away, / but he who gathers money little by little makes it grow.

—*Proverbs 13:11*

Dear Lord,

I got tickled when I gave my nine-year-old son a twenty-dollar bill to go somewhere with specific instructions to spend it wisely. He went to an activity that was supposed to cost only ten dollars, and he came back with just seventy-four cents! It was his first taste of financial freedom, and he lost control.

Now that he is older and has to earn the money we give him, he is much more careful about how he spends it. Please help all of our children be responsible with money. Give them the self-control they need to make wise decisions. May they always remember to tithe immediately, to save a portion, and to avoid spending money that they don't have. Don't let them make the mistake of getting into debt, but if they do, let them learn from it. Help them be wise stewards of the money you have given them. Amen.

OLDEST CHILD

I will pour out my Spirit on your offspring, / and my blessing on your descendants.   *—Isaiah 44:3*

Dear Lord,

He is the first one: the first to teach us the miracle of birth, of being parents, and many other things we never knew we had within us. He has been our inspiration to be better people, to be more of an example of Christ, to do our best, and especially to have more children.

Thank you so much for his precious life. He wants things to be so perfect, but he is constantly frustrated by the interference of his siblings in this goal. Help him enjoy being a kid for as long as he can, and to be patient with those around him. Sow unselfishness in his heart, that he may reap a life filled with joy. Amen.

MIDDLE CHILD

"... everyone who is called by my name, / whom I created for my glory, / whom I formed and made."
—*Isaiah 43:7*

Dear Lord,

Each of them was the youngest for a few years, until another baby came along. And now, neither has the distinction of being the oldest or the youngest. So, where do they fit? This is the question I see my two middle children—one a boy and one a girl—asking themselves. Each wants to be different from the others; both want to know that they are special. They also have to become independent a little sooner because Mommy's attention sometimes is diverted from their needs by the urgent needs of others.

Please let them always know they are loved tremendously and are very special. May they never seek to be different in ways that aren't pleasing to you. Help them find their unique gifts, talents, and abilities and, in the process, draw nearer to you. May I continually remember to encourage them and to let them know what a blessing they are to my life. Amen.

YOUNGEST CHILD

"I will give you ... / riches stored in secret places, so that you may know that I am the LORD, / the God of Israel, who summons you by name."

—Isaiah 45:3

Now that I'm an older parent, I look at my youngest child and cherish all the stages she goes through. I realize that this is the last time I'll witness these little events with my children, such as kindergarten graduation and the victory of a first lost tooth.

Dear Lord, show me the delicate balance between relishing these times and spoiling my child. My other children see how much time I have to spend with her and forget that I did the same for them when they were little. Don't let them be resentful toward her. Let her know that she is very special also, even though she has to put up with getting more hand-me-down clothes than the others ever did! Bless her, and may she glorify you in her valuable life. Amen.

ENCOURAGEMENT

You and I may be mutually encouraged by each other's faith. —*Romans 1:12*

Dear Lord,

Sometimes I get so busy with everyday things that I find myself focusing on what the children are doing wrong and forgetting to encourage them. Help me think of creative, sincere ways to reward them for jobs well done and for good deeds done without being asked. May they know they are appreciated and valued not just for their performance, but for their character traits. In place of a negative comment, help me to think of a positive comment to build them up. Amen.

TEACHERS

And if we know that he hears us—whatever we ask—
we know that we have what we asked of him.
                                      —1 John 5:15

Dear Lord,

I thank you that every year, you hear my prayers
for my children to have the teacher or teachers
they need for every subject. There have been some
years that the children have had teachers I would
not have chosen for them. But you knew what my
children needed when I did not; for instance, you
knew that my daughter needed a "tough," orga-
nized teacher last year to prepare her for middle
school this year.

Thank you for hearing my prayers and for being
faithful to our family. Amen.

Seasoning Their Speech

A gentle answer turns away wrath. —*Proverbs 15:1*

Y ou can get much further with honey than with lemon," my mother used to say. How her homespun wisdom has stuck in my mind through the years! She was right, and as I teach this to my children, I hope they apply this principle to how they communicate with others.

How they relate to others can affect not only their relationships with teachers, friends, siblings, and parents, but also how they someday will relate to their future mate, to their own children, and to their co-workers.

One of the best things I can do for them right now is to train them to relate to other people in a way that reflects grace and strength of character. Please, Lord, give me wisdom in this effort. Amen.

FUTURE OCCUPATION

"I have brought you glory on earth by completing the work you gave me to do." —John 17:4

Dear Lord,

Even though my children may change occupations several times in their lives, I pray that you would begin, even now, to guide them in the activities and classes they will need for their future work.

Help them learn what interests them most. Go before them as they choose a college. May they have a job or jobs that they thoroughly enjoy and that provide well for their families. Let them always glorify you in whatever they do. Amen.

Gifts and Talents

Every good and perfect gift is from above, coming down from the Father of the heavenly lights.

—James 1:17

Dear Lord,

Sometimes when my children realize they are gifted or talented in a particular area, they have to learn not to brag, boast, or become conceited. Yet, I want them to be proud of themselves and their accomplishments.

At other times they struggle with feelings of doubt—*Can I really do this?* At times like these, I not only want to encourage them, but also to let them know that I am truly confident of their abilities.

Help me as a mother to find a balance—to teach them to be confident and yet thankful, knowing that their gifts and talents come from you.

STAYING CONNECTED WITH FRIENDS

I thank my God every time I remember you.
—Philippians 1:3

A few friends of mine and I meet about once every month or two and eat breakfast together. We share how our families are doing, how work is going, and our dreams for the future. We cry with one another, pray for one another, and rejoice in the victories we have in our lives, whether they are large or small.

I also walk about twice a week with a friend with whom I can share day-to-day issues. We're able to bounce ideas off each other and help steer each other through situations we find ourselves in. We also share the hilarious things that happen, and we laugh a lot.

Lord, help me always make time for friendships. Thank you for my friends and for the encouragement and support they are to me. Amen.

Saying No

"For my yoke is easy and my burden is light."
—Matthew 11:30

One of the hardest words for me to say is no. "No, I have other plans." "No, I've got too much on my plate right now." "I'm sorry, but I really can't." "No, but thank you for asking." These are some of the more graceful ways of saying this short but very difficult word.

Help me remember that every time I say yes to something, I'm saying no to some of the other priorities in my life, such as spending time with my family, getting things done in my home, and simply having some leisure time.

May I discern between what is good and what is best, and choose only the best. Let me choose what you really want me to be doing, and do it well. Amen.

BEAUTY

*Your beauty should not come from outward adornment.
. . . Instead, it should be that of your inner self, the
unfading beauty of a gentle and quiet spirit.*

—1 Peter 3:3-4

Dear Lord,

As I approach "the big 4-0," I feel more of a desire
to take care of myself—to eat healthy, exercise reg-
ularly, take care of my skin, drink more water. But
although these things are good, I also don't want to
idolize youth or become obsessed with taking care
of myself. Lord, let me find a healthy balance in all
of these areas.

My daughters are watching to see how I conduct
myself in these matters. I don't want them to worry
about their appearance, but to be thankful for the
way God made them. Let them feel special and beautiful because they are created in your image. Help my
husband and me compliment them for their outward
attributes, but especially for their inward character.

Let me age gracefully and still be a woman who
reflects your beauty and glory, no matter what my
age, shape, or hair color. Thank you that I'm always
lovely to you. Amen.

POPULARITY

"So don't be afraid; you are worth more than many sparrows."   —*Matthew 10:31*

My preteen daughter and I were having our usual bedtime discussion as I tucked her in. "Mom, there are some girls at school who act as if I'm not good enough for them to speak to."

I asked her if they acted like that when they were in a group or by themselves. She had not noticed, so the next time we discussed it, she said, "They are nice to me when they're alone, but they ignore me when they're in a group."

"Do you think you've done something to make them angry?" I asked.

"No," she said.

I asked, "Well, if they act one way around you and another way around their friends, do you think you need friends like that?"

"No," she grinned and gave me a hug.

Lord, please continue to remind me and my daughter that popularity is fleeting, and make it our goal instead to be well thought of and respected. Amen.

PREVENTING
BURNOUT

*"Come to me, all you who are weary and burdened, and
I will give you rest."*   *—Matthew 11:28*

Home Manager" is how I described my job for
eleven years. I cooked the meals, cleaned the
house, and supervised the children. However, as I
began to work part-time, I felt myself becoming
frustrated at not being able to get things done and
the lack of voluntary help from my family. Before
the frustration turned to anger, I asked you, Lord,
to prepare my husband's and my children's hearts
so that they would be willing to rise to the occasion
and help out. They have, but we are still in the
process of making these changes in responsibilities.
Thank you for hearing my prayer for help.

Continue to give us wisdom, patience, and dedi-
cation as we work as a team to take care of our
home and one another. Help us prevent burnout
by keeping ourselves—all of us—flexible and
unselfish. Amen.

FACING A BULLY

*Do not gloat over me, my enemy! / Though I have
fallen, I will rise.* —Micah 7:8

Lord,

I'll never forget the words from my son's lips as
tears streamed down his face. "Pray hard, Mom,
pray hard." He was referring to my offer of prayer
for him as he faced a bully each day at school. As
my son made the decision not to fight back, he was
being ostracized more and more by boys who had
once been his friends. As we prayed for his safety,
for his friendships to stay intact, and for wisdom in
facing these situations with honor without using
violence, I saw you strengthen my child's faith.

The bully was eventually suspended from school.
My son's friends saw how my son had handled
some situations in an admirable way, and we talked
to the teacher in private about the situation. You
abundantly answered our prayer and taught our
family that you are our protector. Thank you, dear
Lord. Amen.

Bullying Others

"First be reconciled to your brother or sister, and then come and offer your gift." —*Matthew 5:24 NRSV*

Dear Lord,

It is hard when I see or hear that my child hurt someone with his words or actions.

Give me wisdom to understand what is going on in his life to cause this. In hurting others, is he trying to fit in with a certain crowd, tearing others down so he will feel better, or just taking advantage of his size to get his way?

Search my heart and let me know if I am modeling this behavior in any way.

Meet my child's needs, soften his heart, and help him face this sin; don't let it take root in his life. Instead, please give him your love for other people. May he be reconciled to those he has wronged. Amen.

BEING TEASED

Do not pay attention to every word people say.
—Ecclesiastes 7:21

Mom, do you think I'm _____?" "No, honey," I gently reply, and then I have the opportunity to genuinely affirm my child. Dear Lord, thank you that my children feel that they can come to me for encouragement when they have been battered verbally by this world. Give me the healing words and sincere compliments that I need to pass on to them.

So many times others try to put my children into boxes and tell them who they are. Don't let them believe the untruthful things others say about them. Let them stand firm in who they are in Christ and know that they are uniquely precious to you. May they embrace the way you made them and be thankful, not resentful. Don't let anything said or implied hinder their faith, damage their spirit, or cause them to compromise their values. If there are some things they should change, give them wisdom as to whether altering that aspect of their lives would be beneficial.

Protect their hearts, Lord. Amen.

Pregnancy

I praise you because I am fearfully and wonderfully made; / your works are wonderful, / I know that full well.   —Psalm 139:14

It is so peaceful and quiet sitting here. I reflect on the tiny miracle growing within me, and once again I am in total awe of you, the Creator. I feel your presence and cherish this moment as your child. Thank you for letting me be a part of your plan for this little person's life.

Keep my baby safe as she grows and develops. Bless this child with a sweet disposition, a gentle nature, and a passion for you. May she desire to do your will above all else, and to be one of your lights to the next generation. When home is far from a peaceful and quiet place, remind me of your presence then too, and the miracle of this precious child's life. Amen.

MULTITASKING

And whatever you do, whether in word or deed, do it all in the name of the Lord Jesus.

—Colossians 3:17

The sayings "I feel as though I'm always putting out fires" or "I'm always flying by the seat of my pants" are common with a couple of my friends. They are referring to the frustration of handling the most urgent matters, things that demand our immediate attention but are not always the most important.

Lord, I thank you that you know how rushed I am sometimes. Help me find pockets of time that I may have overlooked and use them for meal-planning, reading, answering mail, or making important phone calls. Some time that I've "found" has been standing in the checkout line in a store, waiting to pick up my children from school, or waiting during my child's piano lessons.

When I get little "fires" taken care of, I can spend bigger blocks of time basking in the warmth of my family, connecting with friends, or taking on a large task I've been putting off. Help me use my time wisely and spend it on matters of eternal significance. Amen.

Moving

The world and its desire are passing away, but those who do the will of God live forever.

—1 John 2:17 NRSV

Lord,

As our nine-year-old son broke into tears today, I could understand his pain. There is a certain bittersweetness about moving. The other children and I are excited about the new adventures that lie ahead, but a lump forms in my throat when I think of saying good-bye to my dear friends and to all the wonderful acquaintances I've made here.

Bless my husband in his new job and in his relationships with new co-workers. There are so many details to attend to. Don't let things become chaotic, but give me wisdom to prepare our children, especially our nine-year-old son, for what is in store for them.

Comfort them as they say good-bye to friends and the things they love about this place. Go before us as we follow your will for our lives, and surround each of us with Christian friends, a wonderful church family, and good neighbors as we establish roots at our new home. Amen.

FRIENDSHIPS

Whoever walks with the wise becomes wise, but the companion of fools suffers harm.
　　　　　　　　　　　　　　—Proverbs 13:20 NRSV

Don't put all your eggs in one basket," my mother would tell me. This saying related to life in many ways: friendships, boyfriends, jobs, and so on. I learned firsthand what this saying meant when my best friend and I drifted apart my sophomore year in high school. It was a challenge to develop new friendships, because I had not bothered to cultivate many other relationships during the four years she and I were so close. Although I have made many very good friends through the years, I've learned that I need two or three strong Christian girlfriends in whom I can confide.

Lord, I thank you for teaching me this lesson early in life. Reveal to my children people who will stand alongside them and support them. May they be blessed with strong, godly influences and friendships. Also teach them that you are the Friend who will never let them down, and who truly sticks closer than a brother. Amen.

MODELING HONESTY

"Whoever can be trusted with very little can also be trusted with much." —Luke 16:10

My mother had paid a large amount of money for me to attend a Christian camp one summer. We had been shopping that day and were well on our way toward home when she discovered a mistake had been made. As she looked over the receipt, she realized the sales clerk had not charged her for a fairly expensive item. She debated only a few seconds and then asked me to turn the car around so she could go into the store and pay for it. I've never forgotten that incident.

Now, when I am tempted to be dishonest in small ways, I try to remember her example and the fact that young eyes are watching to see how I will handle these situations. To be honest is not always convenient, and it sometimes sets me back in relation to time and money, but the reward is eternal.

Lord, when I am tested in the area of honesty, let me always have the patience and courage to do the right thing and to pass the test, no matter how inconvenient or difficult. May my children always value this virtue and live a life of truthfulness before you and others. Amen.

GRANDPARENTS

"He will renew your life and sustain you in your old age." —Ruth 4:15

My grandmother died when I was eighteen months old, leaving me with no grandparents on my father's side. Mayfield and Dewey quickly took up the slack. They were an elderly couple who lived across the street. They loved me, always encouraged me, and rejoiced in any achievement I attained, no matter how small. They thought I was cute as pie, and I ate it up! I still remember seeing and smelling fresh-cut roses from Mayfield's garden, and watching Dewey crack pecans from their huge tree in the front yard.

My children have both sets of grandparents still living. Even though they live far away, Lord, help me remember how important those relationships are to my children, and to cultivate them by sending pictures, encouraging phone calls, and allowing the children to e-mail their grandparents. Thank you for both my parents and my husband's parents, and for their love for us and for our kids. Amen.

MIDDLE SCHOOL

You will keep in perfect peace / him whose mind is steadfast, / because he trusts in you.

—*Isaiah 26:3*

Dear Lord,

As my child begins middle school today, I confess that I am worried. I worry about him finding all of his classes. If he can't, he might be too embarrassed to ask for directions. (He's a lot like his father!) I worry about him not getting to class on time and not arriving with all of the appropriate supplies he needs for each class. I worry about peer pressure. Will he stand for what is right when tempted? And what about his close friends? Will he have any of his close friends in his classes? Will he make new friends who will encourage him to do what is right and not what is wrong?

Now, I ask you to forgive me for worrying about these things. You are more than capable of watching over my child in all of these areas, including those I haven't thought of and may never know about. I give my concerns to you. Bless my child, and keep him in perfect peace as he takes more and more small steps into adulthood. Thank you, Lord. Amen.

STARTING SCHOOL

Cast all your anxiety on him because he cares for you.
—1 Peter 5:7

The clerk at the grocery store hit the nail on the head. "Your baby just started school today, right?" "How could you tell?" I asked, perplexed at her incredible perception. "I can tell because I've seen women coming through here for the last hour with tears in their eyes. It always happens the first day of school." Then I realized I was not alone. Other mothers either had watched their children skip into class with excitement or had left quickly after peeling their children off their legs. After experiencing the former, I thought, *She's growing up,* as the tears welled up in my eyes.

Lord, thank you for my children's first day of school. Bless their relationships with their teachers, their friends, and other children in their class.

Help them be not afraid to ask questions, and help them understand what is expected of them. May they desire to do their best at all times and form solid friendships that will encourage them. Amen.

Relationship with Dad

As a son with his father he has served with me in the work of the gospel. —*Philippians 2:22*

When our children were younger and my husband traveled quite a bit, I missed him terribly when he was gone. But the children anticipated the very minute their daddy would walk through the door. They would jump up and down and squeal with delight when his car would drive up. Even though he doesn't travel as much now, they still are very happy to see him come through the door at the end of the day.

Lord, I pray that my husband and the children would remain close and that they would respect him, even through their teen years. I pray that they would forgive his mistakes and understand that he truly has their best interests at heart. Give him wisdom in leading our family, disciplining our children, encouraging and blessing them, and showing love to each one in the way they interpret love. Thank you for the fact that he loves you and looks to you as his example. Amen.

Relationships
with Siblings

Live at peace with everyone. —Romans 12:18

I often feel like a referee. Sometimes when I hear "Mom!" called out in the dreaded "I'm gonna tell on somebody" tone, I jokingly hide behind the doorway, which brings a laugh from my children every time.

Lord, you know how I long for my children to love one another, as they should, without selfishness. But that is something we all struggle with, no matter what age. I pray they would be as close as possible and that sibling rivalry would not drive a wedge between any of them. May they be genuinely happy for one another's achievements, respect one another's property and privacy, and be considerate of one another's feelings. As they grow in their relationship with you, help them challenge one another and hold one another accountable in love. Amen.

Holidays

Let your conversation be always full of grace, seasoned with salt, so that you may know how to answer everyone.

—Colossians 4:6

O Lord,
You know how I look forward to the holidays, especially spending time with my husband and children. This year will be very different as my husband's family comes to spend Christmas with us. I love them very much, but some of our traditions are very different from theirs. Give me wisdom in handling delicate situations that may arise, and help me not have unrealistic expectations. May their visit to our home be a relaxing and joy-filled experience. Help me organize well, plan ahead, and be prepared so we can relax and enjoy one another's company. Let us build good memories and strengthen our relationships with them.

May we all remember, no matter how different our customs, the real reason we celebrate Christmas. Thank you for sending your Son, Jesus. Amen.

RELATIONSHIP WITH MOM

But his mother treasured all these things in her heart.
—Luke 2:51

I can only imagine Mary, in her old age, telling her grandchildren about Jesus. How special her relationship with him must have been! What advice does a mother give to God's Son? How intimidating! But I think she probably wasn't intimidated the least bit, and so neither should I be. Just as you handpicked Mary to be the mother of Jesus, you chose me to be the mother of my four beloved children.

Please continue to whisper to my heart the words that will bless my children. Let me pass these words on to them with a hug, a smile, or a sweet kiss on the forehead. When I must point out something that needs to be improved, give me words of grace. Keep me cool during discipline, strong when challenged, soft when encouraging, humble when I make mistakes, and always loving—just like Jesus. Amen.